The secretive soul

Mirela Muresan

Presentation by *BookLeaf Publishing*

Web: www.bookleafpub.com

E-mail: info@bookleafpub.com

ISBN: 9789357615709

First edition 2022

DEDICATION

I'll like to dedicate this book to my beautiful mother, who gave me the wisdom for life and light to lead on in the dark times of life. She has shown me absolutely anything is possible and life is a long hard journey with rewards along the way of each obstacle we come across.

WE LIVE, LEARN, GAIN, LOSE, REPEAT.

Gratitude is the way to look at everything in a positive up note.

ACKNOWLEDGEMENT

Thank you for taking a chance on this book and time as well.

I went into making this book with love.

I hope you have taken something worth remembering from it, it is my first book, progress still in the making. I have a whole heap more to be published but of course everything takes time and dedication.

PREFACE

I may be young at age but not at soul.

Through these few pages, a lot can be felt and seen through the eyes of an old soul.

A few may not understand what it is to be an old soul or even an empath but this book will show a little through what the eyes of an old soul can perceive in this life while being empathetic.

Young or old we all perceive differently and feel differently.

I've learnt a lot and always been that friend who was the parent in the friendships, the mindful, the one who thinks before she speaks and gives motivation speech's as advice.

One thing I wasn't sure about was understanding who I was exactly.

Thankfully poetry existed and I found a way to mend a word or two of how I felt and what I saw.

I only learnt from the best and took what I could and yet I am still in the making of something you can call among the lines of... life

AUTUMN

When it comes to autumn, each tree takes its
own time and reaches its own level in changing,
falling and adapting into the season.
humans are all a mess in every season so
reluctant to change.
complain about no change
only to expect change
it's something I call along the lines of
beauty in the ugliness of seasons.

SHATTERD GRASS

Shadows of my past,
Empty hearts broken,
Like shattered glass,Only to blame my last past
for not seeing the other side of the green grass
without the rain is no grass
without tears our hearts won't last
dear mother let it rain for the dryness will not
last.

LUST DESTRUCTION

3

My lustful thoughts are spiralling out of control
without boundaries,
my mind and body never knew what boundaries
were when with you
It was limitless when it came to you.
It's just a thought I tell myself
Stop
It's a self-made destruction.

BLOOSIM

A flower never thinks to beat the nearest flower
around to grow faster,
each flower has its own pace of growing at its
own potential
Life isn't a timed competition,
yet people act like it's a ticking timebomb.

It's a beauty loop of obstacles we face
Which helps us grow faster for the next obstacle
until we face the beginning of a new cycle.

MOONLIGHT

5

Such kiss with passion and intensity under the
stars and moonlight for that is what I call magic,
while Our souls are tied, our eyes see beyond
earthly aspects we tend to be upbeat now and
then,
that kiss was only magic while it lasted,
as our lips part ways, I can still taste that sweet
masculinity of those soft lips.

ONE TO LOVE

He told me
He loved me
I told him I'm not one to love
I'm not one to forget either.

DYING LOVE

Needed somebody when I had nobody,
got distance when love was needed.
Now I don't have a heart left to give out
nor the energy,

We pour our self until our bottle overflows,
drowns us in the mist of the stormy sea, only
for us to learn to reach sore ourselves and yet to
be okay with going over it again in a
never-ending cycle of dying love.

SOUL TALK

it's on the edge of disappearing into dust,
dead yet alive.
Through my eyes it's
floating into the sky just live above water
feeling the air breeze and watching the birds
surround you with vibrations of love which is so
powerful that can take you back to your inner
child self.
the pure innocence seen from above only saints
will know about.
it comes alive when you can freely touch the
clouds,
but nothing is more magical and screams ALIVE
then being able to touch the stars and drifting
towards the shimmering Moon.

of course, it's all an illusion
but it doesn't hurt to say what if for all.

They told me to wake up and live in reality, little
do they know this to me is all a reality and
forever will be. If it's not, I'll be a dead soul
remaining in a moving body.

LA VIE

9

I'm completely terrified
letting you see me for who I am
layers peeled back all on display from past
trauma to new trauma.
Emotions running hot and cold unable to think
about anything only the blackness in something
we call life.
Some of us don't even call it life.

OLD HOME

My dearest love,

This generation is broken into millions of lost
pieces of course of which cannot or ever will be
found.
tell me what happened to pen and paper, the
quill and fresh ink, the white dove and pigeon
delivering our messages back and forth.
The secret dates and rainy dances when no one
would watch us.
Tell me where did it all go. these past years felt
like a decade and counting
My soul won't be at ease much longer until my
soul is at rest because it's too much to take
without another soul like this.
It was supposed to be Called home, old home.
Not anymore…

SOUL

Your soul is haunting me for a love so powerful
we yet have to experience.

REGRET

My soul burns and my eyes flood with tears of passion when thinking about the one I loved so deeply, now it's a past love but one love that will never come by again.
hold tight to the ones dearest their only with you once until they vanish into eternity.

WITH YOU

With you time was never lost but regained,
With you hours felt like minutes,
With you climbing mountains wasn't a problem
With you peace started
With you it started,
With you it will end

MIDNIGHT

He was like the midnight sky, unreachable but
yet beauty couldn't come down on him.
Stars wonder around him and kept him afloat,
even with hundreds of stars loneliness was still
buried deep in the middle of his soul.
But through his eyes all you saw was a sky lit
full of stars
One would wonder how possibly could someone
be lonely with that many stars?

OCEAN BATTLES

If sacrificing my serenity to go through oceans
and battles of never ending tides and waves for
your heart to never miss a beat,
I'll be at battle everyday until my last drop of
tears and breath are met.
Love is not to be given up on but only to be seen
out as something worth fighting for and hoping
with all faith the love will stand above water
even after many fights and obstacles that
intertwine.

GIFTS

It took years to understand
The light and dark are equally both gifts in life
which goodness can be collect from,
The wise will have gained wisdom,
While the utterly mindless ones will gain doubt
and renter the dark.
Take the dark and turn it into light.

TARNISH

17

Heart locket tarnished,
Once you tarnish they won't look at you with
such value no more
There's no worth you end up being contempt to
their eyes
But plate it with a gold finish and you'll be the
centre of attention once again.

real or plated they'll love you for the outside of
the value but what truely holds such value to you
is your history of what's inside that locket.

ESCAPE

I brought a new book...
Or two, maybe three
Just for the escape of this woeful contempt
world of what people call "life"
For an hour or two my mind can travel away
Have a ticket away from sadness and affliction
Have a ticket to contentedness
Can't forget the...
Cup of bitter Carmel coffee
Notebook pages stained with coffee and
cigarettes scents and bourbon.

CHILDLIKE VS. CHILDISH

Sunny day,
Sunny wind,
Summer day,
Laughter and joy fill the air
her smiling eyes,
Hard to miss,
But hard to forget,
Like a blueprint
A beautiful rare young child enjoying the
midnight sky of summer breeze.

A SPECTRUM OF FEAR

Sparks of illusions is all it is. A contentment heart will be able to unravel it to its finest myth. But a discontentment heart will only be stuck in the rewinding spark of illusions of mirrors that cannot be escaped within or out.
Only those with an open heart and white light of what I call wisdom can break this illusion which is the spectrum of fear.

BURIED ALIVE

21

You'll try to make talk but get thrown into the deepest
grave,
with only some fresh soil thrown over you to cover
your words used to express yourself.
You will be stripped of your voice, thoughts and
heart.
it's what they do best.
they bury you alive before your death date......